THE TURTLE
and
THE LION

THE TURTLE

and

THE LION

*Lessons for Living while
Learning to Play the Piano*

by

MARSHA MARTIN

Charleston, SC

www.PalmettoPublishing.com

THE TURTLE and THE LION:

Lessons for Living while Learning to Play the Piano

Copyright © 2021 by Marsha Martin

First Edition

Hardcover ISBN: 978-1-7378184-0-3
Paperback ISBN: 978-1-7378184-1-0
eBook ISBN: 978-1-7378184-2-7

DEDICATION

For Mama and Deedee

and

my piano students and chorus members

through all these 'musical' years

CONTENTS

PRELUDE

Why a Turtle and a Lion? What do they have to do with piano lessons?

Years ago, before the turn of the millennium, I was told that there were inmates at one of our local correctional institutions (commonly known as a prison) who had requested a music theory class, and I was asked if I would consider teaching such a class. (They had my name because a decade or so before that I had started and directed a choir at the same prison.)

I was interested and began work on the required syllabus and necessary forms to submit to the state Department of Corrections for approval. After all the required hoops had been jumped through, the class actually began with a few men who wanted to learn some music theory and how to play the keyboard – or at least were curious about it.

Early on in the classes I realized that the men had a very unrealistic idea of how long it would take to learn to play the piano. So one Saturday morning I took a small stuffed turtle to class and introduced him as "Patience", telling them that that is what it would take to become proficient at the piano.

A few weeks after that, one of the students (a man who was in on a murder charge) told me that we needed a lion because, as he said, it also takes courage to learn to play the piano. That led me to a search for a Beanie Baby lion to match our Beanie Baby turtle. (That is itself another story for another time.) Several weeks later I was happy to take "Courage" to class to join "Patience" as our class mascots and inspiration. To this day "Patience" and "Courage" reside on the left and right ends of the keyboard at every class and are introduced to any newcomer who joins us.

Seeing how important "Patience" and "Courage" were to my students at the prison, I started placing them on my Steinway grand in my home studio – the turtle on the left of the music rack and the lion on the right. They still reside there (except on Saturday mornings) – for the benefit of my adult students as much or maybe even more than for my young students. The more involved someone gets in their music pursuit, the more relevant "Patience" and "Courage" become.

So, it seems appropriate that "Patience" and "Courage" serve as the title and inspiration for this book being written for the benefit of adults learning to play the piano.

INTRODUCTION

For most adults just making the decision to start piano lessons requires Courage. The voice inside their head is saying things like:

> ➢ Where did you get such an idea?

> ➢ What makes you think you can do that?
> What if you don't have any talent?

> ➢ Don't you have better things to do with your time and money?

> ➢ Won't you feel silly being a beginner at your age?

> ➢ What will your family (spouse, kids, grandkids, siblings, friends, neighbors, co-workers) think?! What will they say?!

> ➢ Why don't you just listen to more music – or go to some concerts?

> ➢ What teacher would want you as a student?

The common lurking question haunting a would-be adult beginner is: "What if I just don't have any musical talent?" So they figure they will start lessons as a way to get their question answered. They will try it for a while and if things don't go as well as they think they should, they will have proof that, as they feared, they just weren't born with the talent necessary to do music. And they will quit lessons knowing that it just wasn't meant for them, but at least they tried and now, sadly, they know.

When an adult student asks me that question or some-times even before they verbalize it (but I can tell it is the "elephant in the room"), I answer them with quotes from two of my favorite musician-authors: Dr. Shinichi Suzuki and Dr. Oliver Sacks.

Dr. Suzuki is famous for the music education method he created and spread worldwide known as the International Suzuki Method. His method is used successfully with children beginning as young as age two or three. Dr. Suzuki believed that music is everyone's native language, that everyone can learn to make music just as they inevitably learn to speak their mother tongue. His premise was that musical talent is something that can be developed in any child (adult!).

So that is where "Patience" comes in. It is not about who has inherent talent, but rather who simply has patience to stick with it – just as they had to do in order to learn English (i.e., their native language).

By the way, I will mention here (because we will get to this later on) that Shinichi Suzuki said he was not trying to create a world of professional musicians but rather trying to spread a philosophy for living that would open up a world of beauty for people so that they would have greater enjoyment in their lives.

Dr. Oliver Sacks, an internationally famous neurologist, was an enthusiastic amateur pianist and thus was especially interested in music and the brain. You have probably heard of him because he was the subject of the well-known movie "Awakenings" or maybe because of the Nova episode "Musical Minds" on PBS.

In his book *Musicophilia: Tales of Music and the Brain* he tells us a lot about how humans are able to make music. Music occupies more areas of our brain than language does. Humans are a musical species. I even seem to remember him saying that there are more parts of the human body and brain made to make music than to do any other human activity! In other words, we are beings created to "make" music – not just to listen to and like music, but to MAKE music! Think about it; it takes a while for that to soak in.

So back to our beginning adult piano student's question and my resolute answer: You have all the physical and mental and emotional equipment, and the necessary "talent" to MAKE MUSIC. You just have to make friends with "Patience" and "Courage" and get going!

♪ ♪ ♪ ♪ ♪

Music (a melody) is built on a succession of pitches known as a scale, and the chords that underlie, support, and enhance that melody are tied to the steps in the scale. So, it seemed appropriate to organize the thoughts in this book on the steps in the musical scale.

ONE-OCTAVE MAJOR SCALE OF CHAPTERS

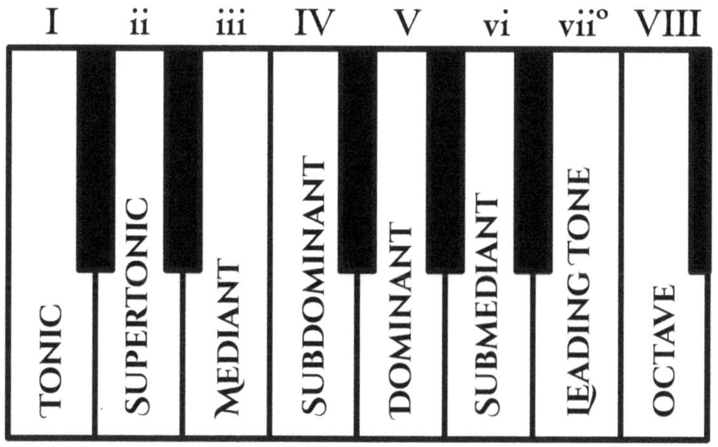
I
ii
iii
IV
V
vi
vii°
VIII
TONIC
SUPERTONIC
MEDIANT
SUBDOMINANT
DOMINANT
SUBMEDIANT
LEADING TONE
OCTAVE

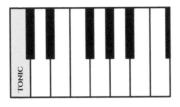

I

VALUES – PRIORITIES

Continuity – Quality – Sharing Beauty –
Vision – Learning – Equality – Higher Road

Appropriately, we will begin our journey, our "non-song with words," at the first note of our scale, on the Tonic. That is the tone that we keep hearing, the note and chord that determines where the piece resides, where we feel most comfortable. It is at the root of the song's identity. It is "Home". So this chapter is about our Values and Priorities, what makes us who we are and gives us our identity.

The most basic necessity in Music is CONTINU-ITY. As performers we are obligated above all else to keep going. Our listeners will forgive us for mistakes but not for quitting. If something unexpected happens (i.e., we make some 'horrible' mistake, God forbid!), we have to recover, improvise, do something…but we cannot stop, give up, quit, get up from the piano and walk off!

That is certainly a Life Lesson that most of us have learned and ascribe to. Although we would not consider actually ending our life when things don't go as we planned or when we make a horrible mistake, nonetheless there are many other ways that we can give up, quit, walk away. Think about a time when you didn't have the patience or courage to stick with your task, your vision, your dream and just gave up on it, did something different, changed the subject.

Performing music, or even just seriously practicing music, forces us over and over again to practice "Not quitting". That is where our lion "Courage" comes in – courage to keep going when we would rather run away – from others, from ourselves, from the situation. For the sake of something we value (learning to play the piano or this particular piece) we bravely put ourselves into a situation where we now will face that dilemma over and over again. But we have chosen our priorities, and we are determined to stick with it, scary though it can be.

The next highest value that we learn from our music is that QUALITY is by far more important than sheer quantity. A piece of music moves us by how beautiful it is, what it says to us, how it makes us feel. It can be long or short; that is not what makes the difference. It can have a lot of notes or only a relative few.

How many people use up their time, their energy, their emotions, their abilities going after Quantity: impressive salary, large house, expensive car, numerous titles after their name, big bank account, number of Boards they serve on, number of friends they have on Facebook, and on and on? And yet none of those guarantee that their life is happy and fulfilled. It is the Quality of the life they live that determines that.

We can whip through a number of pieces, learning the obvious things like the notes and rhythm, and think that we have done it. But we have robbed ourselves, and anyone who might hear us play those pieces, of the real beauty and deep meaning in the music. What could have made a lasting impression, one that might have inspired us, has simply come and gone hardly to be thought of again.

Working at each musical skill until we attain a certain level of mastery requires determination and our other mascot "Patience". That kind of mastery allows us to attain Quality, Beauty. Quality is not about how much we can get done in the shortest amount of time. Quality is about how deep we can go in any amount of time.

Quality is Beauty. If the tone isn't beautiful, the music memorable, it does not matter how flashy or impressive we try to be. Music demonstrates that Beauty and Meaning are more important than showing off what we can do, how many notes we can play, how fast we can go.

Think about people you have known who tried to impress you by their snazzy clothes, their shiny fast car, their bragging about all their big accomplishments. I remember some of the quiet, less obviously remarkable young people in my high school class who at class reunions years later were the ones who had done deeds of great value in the world (still without showiness).

Quality over quantity plays out in a number of ways. But it is a value that we must choose and then prioritize. Music gives us that choice to make at every small incremental stage of our musical development and in learning each individual piece. Over and over we have to decide to go for Quality.

After consistently making that choice in our music, that kind of thinking, of prioritizing, can begin moving into everyday decisions we are making in our lives, reminding us that it is the quality of what we are doing that matters the most. It is so easy to fall into the trap of thinking we are better because we are busier, because we are cramming more things into each day, checking more things off on our to-do list. That in itself doesn't prove anything; that is sheer quantity of activity. We must apply the Quality standard to evaluate the worth of what we are doing. Our music teaches us that in real, audible ways, giving us memories that inspire and last.

If we value Quality (Beauty) and make it a priority, we also realize that BEAUTY NEEDS TO BE SHARED. How many times when you have seen an astounding rainbow or a beautiful sunset or a magnificent flower in bloom or a bird you have never seen before have you wished your spouse or friend was there to see it with you? It is a normal human reaction to want to share something beautiful, something awe-inspiring. It is the same with the music we make; it is to be shared.

This is where I often hear things like this from my adult piano students: "I'm not trying to become a concert pianist. I don't want to perform; I just want to play for myself, for my own enjoyment. I would be far too nervous to play for anyone else. And besides, I'm not that good. They wouldn't want to hear me anyway."

Let's bring in our friend "Courage" to sit beside you during this conversation because the voices speaking just now were Fear and Ego. Being overly concerned about our own ego keeps us from sharing something meaningful with friends and from taking risks that would propel us forward to becoming better musicians. (We will continue this important conversation later on.)

The Life Lesson here is that sharing beauty and meaning with people, especially those we love, is more important than protecting our sometimes too-fragile ego.

Related to that is the necessity of setting our goals, whether in Music or in Life, based on our own inner VISION. That is not to say that we already know it all. One of the things we learn rather quickly when we start taking music lessons is how much there is to learn from the succession of musicians/teachers who have gone before us. (Music cannot be done in depth from Do-It-Yourself books.) But we can't simply try to reproduce what these great pianists before us have done. We have to learn from them and then take it inside ourselves, make it ours. Playing beautiful, meaningful, inspiring music requires following our aural and spiritual vision. Just as in life we need to have a vision of what it is we want with our whole being, in order to accomplish our goal, our unique gift to the world.

An obvious and assumed, but as yet unmentioned, value in this undertaking of learning to play music is that of LEARNING AND GROWING. We value lifelong learning and believe that we are never too old to learn or we wouldn't have ever considered taking music lessons as an adult.

It is always interesting to hear the responses my adult piano students get from friends and colleagues when they tell them they are taking lessons. Some are really surprised, "What?! You've got to be kidding! Why at your age are you doing something like that?!" Those are the ones who don't value lifelong learning or at least not enough to muster up the courage to give it a try themselves.

But frankly those people are in the small minority. The more likely response is, "Oh, that is fabulous! When did you start? What's it like? I've thought of doing something like that myself but figured that was a silly notion. Maybe it's not so silly after all. Tell me all about it! When can I hear you play something?" The excitement and shared joy is incredible. Taking lessons is not only a gift to yourself, it is a gift to all the people who know you: to your peers because it encourages them to follow their secret dream, whatever it is; and to your own children, grandchildren, or other young people because it is a real-life example to them that learning is for all ages!

One of the incredible things that music does so well is bring disparate, diverse people together. Music ignores age, sex, race, income, politics, and other familiar barriers between people. It is an equalizer turning fellow musicians into peers, friends, people sharing a similar purpose and goal. Music promotes the value of EQUALITY in a way that nothing else can.

There are so many examples of this, all of them wonderful and inspiring. One dramatic example is the Divan Orchestra for young people. It was started in 1999 by the Jewish conductor Daniel Barenboim and the Palestinian academic Edward Said. Its goal is to promote friendship and dialogue between Israelis and Palestinians, Jews and Arabs.

I myself thank music for bringing me into meaningful friendships with people of other ages, races, ethnic backgrounds, gender preferences, religions – friendships that would never have come about except through music. My music class at the prison is one of those examples of making friends thanks to music.

For me, getting to know people different from myself and to learn from them and expand my understanding and sensitivities is an important value and a priority in my life. This is one way that I believe we can all work for Peace in our little corner of the world. Thank you, MUSIC!

The final value we will talk about here at "home" on our Tonic is that of choosing to take the HIGHER ROAD. As with almost everything in life, music comes in diametrically different types, levels. It can be trivialized, bastardized, vulgarized; it can be used to make money, to start wars, to promote self-harming behaviors, to encourage hate and division. So we must choose which level, which path: higher or lower.

> *Two roads diverged in a wood, and I –*
> *I took the one less traveled by,*
> *And that has made all the difference.*

Choose the Higher Road, in music and in your life, and it will indeed make all the difference. Your life will have Beauty and Meaning.

♪ ♪ ♪ ♪ ♪

II

How to Study and Learn – Work Habits – Process – How to Succeed

Seed-planting – Path of Progress – Detective Work –
Master Teacher/Apprentice – Good Habits –
Prioritizing – No Procrastination – Time Management –
One Task at a time, hardest first – Hard Work pleasant –
Celebrate success at every incremental step

Now we are beginning our second chapter, the second step in our musical scale known as the Supertonic because it is above the tonic. As in starting any journey we need to leave home with a plan. So the things we are going to talk about now are how to study and learn, the process, our work habits, how to proceed so as to reach our goal. (Others would probably entitle a chapter like this "How to Succeed".)

We want our journey toward learning to play the piano to be as positive as possible and not be fraught with mishaps and delays that not only slow us down but can be discouraging. So the way we proceed, the path we choose, is important, beginning with the proper attitude and expectations. And let me say that we definitely need to invite our Turtle friend "Patience" to be our traveling companion.

One of the hardest facts to deal with is that learning to play the piano (like becoming fluent in a foreign language) is not going to happen overnight. It is going to take longer than you thought or hoped, longer than the "ten easy lessons" promised by an over-zealous keyboard salesman throwing in ten free lessons when you buy an instrument from him.

I invite you to envision a beautiful flower garden of your favorite flowers. You plant the seeds one day, but you know not to expect a gorgeous rose bush full of nice-smelling roses the very next day. You faithfully water and feed and weed with the expectation that with the right amount of sun and rain and time, your long-anticipated roses will bloom.

Practicing is like that: you keep working, tending to all the practical details day by day, one practice session after another, with the expectation that when those "seeds" have developed to the proper stage that you will "hear" a beautiful flower. There is no reason for discouragement or doubt along the way! It **will** happen in due time if you just remain faithful, hopeful, diligent...and patient. Your music will bloom, and you will be so happy and proud.

Another expectation we need to talk about is that in much learning, not just in the field of music, progress is not always in a steady onward and upward line. Often we cannot see that our practice today has improved over what we were doing yesterday in the same place, on the same piece. We may not notice a marked improvement over the course of several days. In fact, in may seem as though, in spite of all our good, careful work, that we actually got worse, went backwards! (We need both our friends "Patience" and "Courage" with us in those times.) This is when we have to call on our garden image and muster up our "faith" that assures us that if we just keep doing what we know we need to do that we will get over this hurdle and will reach our goal (possibly many hurdles later).

If we keep our positive attitude and never forget what we learned from Dr. Suzuki and Dr. Sacks, then instead of giving in to discouragement we can view this as a rewarding challenge.

Practice is Problem-Solving and requires bringing in the Detective Agency. Of course, you are the lead detective on the case. If something is not going well, we need to pinpoint just where the problem is and then determine exactly what is causing the problem. Is it fingering, is it a faulty touch, is it not seeing the gesture, the grouping of the notes? Is it not knowing the chord structure right there, or not yet having a vision of the composer's intention in this passage? What is it? Once you have identified the root of the problem, then you need to figure out how to fix it. This is where a good teacher is invaluable because until you have had a lot of experience, you won't have all the resources at your command which would allow you to know just what might do the trick.

To correct mistakes: Detective work…
- ➤ figure out what is wrong
- ➤ analyze why it was wrong; what caused it
- ➤ come up with common sense, practical solutions
- ➤ practice, drill it until correct habits are formed (MUCH repetition)

Patience. Persistence.
"Perfect practice makes perfect"

Just as with any good detective, you need to keep a piano journal in which you keep track of your 'research', i.e., your problem spots, what you think is causing the problem, what you have tried, what has helped and what didn't, what questions you have. You and your teacher are a team, and the more information you provide, the more efficient the team will become.

Let's interrupt this detective work a moment to say a little more about this aspect of learning to play the piano, i.e., the necessity of having the guidance, mentorship of a qualified piano teacher. Learning to play the piano really well and artistically cannot be done in a self-taught situation with teach-yourself books or online videos. The most important things have to be demonstrated and taught one-on-one like an old-world craft being passed down from one generation to the next, from master to apprentice.

That is why you will often read in a biography of a famous pianist you have gone to hear at Symphony Hall or Carnegie Hall or some other well-known performance venue not the music degrees they have but rather the list of the teachers with whom they have studied. Often that list will be a musical genealogy that traces back one pianist-teacher at a time back to some famous 19th century pianist, perhaps even to Liszt or Beethoven! Isn't it nice to have something in this age of computers, robots, and all kinds of incredible technology that still requires personal interaction at a deep and sustained level?

Building good habits in music, as in other things in our lives, requires repetition. But with music it is more repetitions than you would ever imagine; ten times *may* improve a passage, but more realistically it may take 100, or even 1,000 (really).

And of course while you are doing all those repetitions, you must make sure you are doing them correctly. We've all heard the old adage "Practice makes perfect." But that is only if the practice itself was being done accurately, carefully, deliberately. In other words, "PERFECT practice makes perfect!" So be observant and smart in developing good, beneficial habits, not bad ones.

While we are speaking of familiar adages, here is another one we have heard many more times than we can count, "Haste makes waste!" That proves itself time and time again with our music-making. Take the time to do the task right to begin with because trying to undo something or breaking a bad habit takes much longer and is very discouraging! (And our first aural impressions sometimes can never be totally erased.)

Practicing means problem-solving (being that detective we talked about), but it is important not to try to fix all the problems at once. We need to focus on one thing at a time (a key element in Dr. Suzuki's method). Prioritize the problems to be solved and then tackle them one at a time using the outline above. It is important that you identify and tackle the hardest, most daunting tasks first! Doesn't it make sense to start soonest on the ones that are going to require the most time? Our Lion is helpful with this because we often procrastinate on dealing with the things we fear or dread the most. Music gives us practice at not procrastinating!

We can't talk about practicing and developing reliable work habits without mentioning the time problem all adult students have. Now I am not referring to musical time, rhythm, but to actual clock time. As a decades long piano teacher, I have never had an adult call to inquire about piano lessons say that they had a lot of free time and that they were just trying to think of things they might enjoy doing to fill it up. That is not the case with working adults, or stay-at-home parents, or even so-called retired people. The people who are interested in playing the piano are busy, vibrant, engaged and are already committed to many jobs, volunteer services, community activities. So finding time to practice the piano is always an issue.

One of the jobs I take very seriously as their piano teacher is working with them on time management, how to find (make) the time to practice. (That could be a topic for a separate book.) The single piece of advice I will include here is this: Don't wait until you have a huge block of time. Catch little 5, 10, 15-minute intervals to practice one small detail. Make use of small amounts of time that would otherwise be unnoticed (wasted, lost) time. Some days your life activities and commitments seem to conspire to wipe out that hour you had planned to spend at the piano. Don't despair. Just grab those 10 minutes waiting for that phone call to be returned or the 15 minutes until the rice is finished cooking or the 5 minutes until you need to drive your child to their soccer practice. You hear what I am saying. Don't tell yourself, "Well, I would like to practice but there isn't enough time now. I would just be getting started when I'd have to leave."

The trick here is that you must have places already identified that could benefit from five or ten minutes of concentrated work. At lessons I mark such 'dot spots' with a small colored stick-on dot, so that the minute the person opens their music they see it and can go right to it. Otherwise they could spend their five minutes just trying to figure out what to do! Such 'dot spots' need to be short, possibly only one to four measures. If it is a fingering to be fixed for instance, then five minutes on one measure with the right fingering can mean a number of repetitions and a noticeable improvement.

A little story: I had an adult student several years ago who practiced during every TV commercial, believe it or not. That meant she was getting in about fifteen minutes of practice every hour that she watched her favorite television programs. That was just "free" time added on to the time she set aside for practicing. (She made great progress as a beginner.) I am not necessarily endorsing that particular solution to your time problem but just showing you how you can make small amounts of time work for you, and to encourage you to be creative not only with your piano playing but with your time management as well.

All of the things we learn from good piano practicing are invaluable in dealing with our jobs, tasks, assignments that we face in our everyday life. Certainly increased self-discipline, will power, prioritizing, and planning can make many things we do more efficient, less burdensome, and more pleasant.

Our piano practice teaches us that hard work can be pleasurable and something to look forward to and to be grateful for, not to dread or procrastinate. Perhaps a bit of that attitude applied to some of our other time commitments would make them more pleasant as well – just a thought.

Remember: Anything in life, as in music, can be handled if it is reduced to the smallest task! A tiny task done VERY slowly and carefully and calmly with NO stress or anxiety or feeling of being in a hurry is doable. Add those together and you eventually (when the time is right) will arrive at your goal.

And before we leave our Supertonic degree of the scale: The journey is just beginning. Enjoy each incremental stage along the way, appreciating what you are seeing (hearing), what you are learning, what you are accomplishing…and those with you on your journey. Don't save all of your good warm, positive feelings for the end of the journey. Celebrate each day, each stage, each success! Applaud yourself and take a well-deserved bow!

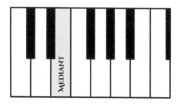

III

PERSONAL CHARACTER

Positive Attitude – Balance – Humility – Vision –
Inner Callings – Sacrifice – Care of Ourselves –
Sharpening your Brain – Listening – Humor

The third degree or step of our scale, the Mediant gets its name from the Latin word which means "middle". While it is not the middle of the scale, it is called that because it is the middle note of the triad (chord) built on the first note of the scale. Just as the Tonic (first) note of the scale is the most important, the one that is the identity for the scale or piece of music we are playing, so is the chord starting on that first note the most important chord in the piece. If the first note of the scale is C and our piece is in the key of C, we are going to hear more C notes and C chords than any others in that piece.

Another name for a chord is triad because it is comprised of three notes. Each note is a skip away; so a C chord is C and E and G. It is the middle note of that chord that determines whether the chord has a major sound or a minor sound. Major versus minor is a big deal in music. A listener may not know the name of it, but they will sure know how they feel. To be simplistic let's just say the difference between major and minor is like the difference between a sunny or a cloudy day, between Yes or No, between energetic or thoughtful. Anyway, a big difference! And it is the middle note, the Mediant, that makes the difference; the other two notes remain the same. So in this Mediant chapter we are going to deal with personal character since that makes a huge difference in the kind of person someone is, the way they play their music, live their life.

Let's begin with an assumption that all beginning adult piano students seem to have, i.e., that it would have been much easier and that they would have learned much faster as a child. They start off feeling like they have a learning handicap because they are 'old'. I point out that they actually have many advantages:

➢ Their coordination is more developed, much more than a very young child.

➢ They already understand the concept of fractions (some children haven't had that in school math yet).

➢ They have had years to develop study and work habits.

➢ They are more responsible.

➢ They have chosen to do this, are not being made to take piano lessons.

➢ They can select their own instrument.

➢ Depending on the particular person, they may have heard much more good music and know something of the great composers (not always the case, as with some of my inmate students).

➢ Their spiritual nature is likely more mature.
(There are others, but let's stop at that.)

I tell them that IF they are in any way at a disadvantage that it is in the realm of psychology. A child doesn't spend time worrying about whether they can play the piano; they just start learning. They can have times when they experience the same impatience, frustration, and even discouragement, but they don't worry about it and agonize over whether they have what it takes or not. They just want it to happen faster. They are in learning mode for everything in life and don't yet know what it feels like to have mastery, control over something.

If I can keep an adult from erecting their psychological brick wall or help them take it down quickly, then they have no learning disability compared to themselves as a child and we can move forward in joy without anxiety.

Isn't this true with other things we set out to do as adults, if we begin with a POSITIVE ATTITUDE believing in ourselves and assuming we can do it, then we already have a very good chance of accomplishing it? A positive attitude says so much about who we are and what we will do in (with) our life!

As we have already mentioned, you have the "talent" necessary to play the piano. Having an I-can-do-it attitude and sticking to it are the most important prerequisites for meeting your goal of learning to play the piano. Perseverance and Faithfulness pay off, in music and in life.

Another psychological aspect of an adult beginner is that they have experienced what it feels like to have a certain degree of knowledge, control, mastery over at least one field, their career, their job. And perhaps it has been a long time since they tried to learn something totally new to them. They are not used to feeling stupid, clumsy, slow, bumbling, insufficient, not in control.

In fact, it is often people with the highest IQ or the PhD or the CEO title (the most "successful" by society's measuring stick) that have the hardest time adjusting to the new condition of being a beginner and the psychology that goes along with that. We have to admit that we don't know this and that being competent or excelling at our job doesn't automatically transfer over to this totally new field of endeavor. It is a challenge to one's ego and self-esteem and is all very humbling, to say the least. This requires a good amount of internal Courage. Developing this kind of courage may pay off in unexpected ways in other areas of our life.

One of the big issues we deal with in music is called BALANCE. That is knowing which hand (or which part of our hand) is playing the melody, the main tune of the piece, and which hand is playing the accompaniment, the back-up. Obviously, it is the melody that needs to be louder so it can be heard, and the accompaniment needs to be softer so as to enhance but not cover up the melody. It takes discernment, careful listening, flexibility, and skill to manage Balance properly in a piece. And of course, the balance can change back and forth between hands (fingers), often quite rapidly. Achieving the proper balance is essential to creating a beautiful performance. (You can imagine what an issue Balance is when making music with other musicians in a chamber group or larger ensemble.)

Balance in music can serve as a wonderful role model for our life: in our experiences, in our prioritizing and making choices, and in our relationships. Knowing when to lead and when to follow, when to step forward and take charge vs. when to step back and do our best supporting and enhancing the one in the spotlight at the moment. Actually that is one definition of the word "humility".

Humility can be a powerful game changer in relationships and opportunities, and in the way we experience life. I would suggest that it is just as important in life as it is in music.

We experience HUMILITY in another way in music also. We admit that we don't know all there is to know about music and about playing the piano and that we never will, no matter how much we practice, play, study, listen. And we can never claim that our rendition of the piece of music we are playing is the only viable way to play it. We study composers, and styles, and periods, and customs, and history, and instrument-making and everything we can pertaining to our piece, and that gets us into an acceptable level of an authentic performance.

But there are others who have also reached that level. And no one can claim theirs is right and all the others equally researched and polished are wrong. Such humility that recognizes we don't have to be the one on top, the Winner, while claiming the others are Losers would go a long way in promoting Peace in our world. In music we can experience all being "winners". Think of an inspired performance of Beethoven's Ninth Symphony in which players and listeners alike are transported to some heavenly realm. Each orchestra musician, each singer, the conductor, every member of the audience are all "winners"! No one is right and all others wrong. All are important (at any one time some as leaders and some as followers). There is give and take, cooperation, unity in diversity, and the result is Beauty.

Making music ourselves and making music a deep part of our life can enrich and expand us beyond the everyday world.

In music and in life we need to set our goals based on VISION and that Vision needs to be of a higher nature than trying to impress our peers. Our focus needs to be on playing beautiful music and communicating inner feelings. If we focus on what others are thinking about us, the music we are creating loses its authenticity and emotional power. It is true that sharing our music with others takes some Courage, but remember that you are the conduit; it should not be self-aggrandizement. In life if we are working for an important cause, we want the focus to be on the cause and the good we are trying to accomplish, not on us and making our name known.

One of the most important decisions we make in life is deciding what career to pursue, and it is usually best if that decision is made by us and not already laid out for us by our family. Interestingly the same is true for our choice of musical instrument we decide to learn to play. I have had adults say to me that their parents wanted them to play, say violin and enrolled them in violin lessons but they just never took to it; what they really wanted was to learn to play the piano. And now many years later they are finally following their inner instinct.

I was at a concert years ago that featured an amazing harpist. In the performer bio it said that she had been a pianist who in her last year of music conservatory signed up for some lessons on harp just to see what it was like. Much to her surprise and the chagrin of her piano teacher, she fell in love with the sound and feel of the harp and changed instruments. It was a case of musical "love at first sight" and finding her musical "soul mate".

Children and people of all ages really can be drawn to a particular instrument and feel an inner connection that they can't explain. Parents often assume it is a passing fantasy maybe because the child's best friend plays that instrument, and sometimes that is the case. But often it is a serious "calling" that ought to be listened to. So music encourages us to listen to those INNER CALLINGS, regardless of the subject matter.

While we are speaking of instruments, making an investment in a worthy instrument, one that will allow you to reach to the heights is extremely important. Often we stick with a poor piano (or a keyboard!) because of the money we would need to invest in upgrading. If we honestly have no financial choice right now, then we stick with what we have and do the best we can to play beautiful music on it. (I myself grew up with a big old upright piano that was passed on to me by my aunt and hauled down to our town in an open trailer hitched to the back of their old station wagon!)

But if there is any way that you can budget your finances differently or save money in a "piano fund", then do it; it is worth it. Don't undervalue yourself and your love of music and of playing the piano. Don't say things like, "It's not that I am this great pianist and need a fabulous piano!" Your time and effort and love of music are of utmost significance. You do deserve an instrument worthy of your desire to play and share beautiful music. If making a substantial financial investment requires prioritizing and perhaps some sacrifices, then that can also be good. SACRIFICE can have lasting rewards in music and in life.

Being serious about playing the piano encourages (even requires) us to take good CARE OF OUR BODY: nutrition, sleep, no abuse of drugs or alcohol, deep breathing, clear head…not because someone is telling us to but because we realize that to do what we want with our music requires us to be at our physical and mental best.

Playing music requires "multitasking" to a degree immeasurable. The first published use of the word "multitask" appeared in an IBM paper describing the capabilities of the IBM System/360 in 1965. The term has since been applied to human tasks, referring to a person dealing with multiple tasks simultaneously. Musicians have been "multitasking" for centuries (millenniums?). Even the most recognized neurologists cannot fully explain how musicians are able to do some of the things they do, e. g. memorizing a Beethoven piano concerto or a four-voice fugue by Bach.

Your devoted music practicing is SHARPENING YOUR BRAIN and having lasting effects in all aspects of your life. (There is a lot of evidence now that practicing and playing music regularly may even stave off the feared onset of Alzheimer's disease.)

In addition to Humility, another personal character quality necessary in music that I feel has a huge bearing on the kind of person we are and the quality of our life is that of LISTENING... and the two are certainly related. Listening and the quality of our listening determines our 'success' as a musician. Repeatedly I hear lectures by world-class pianist-teachers who adamantly state that the level a pianist (any musician) reaches is determined ultimately by the quality of their listening and what they hear! From the very first lesson with a piano student, I tell them we are training their hands, their eyes, their brain, and **their ears**. It comes as a continuing revelation to people with no hearing problem that the longer they do music, the more they are hearing.

Listening in our society is not particularly valued or developed, with the exception of certain categories of people. For instance, I know naturalists who can identify birds by their calls, a skill I have never developed. That requires listening at a deeper, more intent level. Good counselors work to listen carefully and try to "hear" between the lines. And there are other examples.

But generally, when people are in a conversation, one is talking and the other is just trying to formulate what their response is going to be. Sometimes when we are listening to someone on the phone, we realize we just missed their whole last paragraph because our mind wandered somewhere else.

Music requires non-stop careful listening with no distractions, and that requires determination, brain control, and practice. And it is not just knowing how to listen and being able to do that uninterruptedly, but we also need to know what to listen for and understand exactly what it is that we are hearing. That requires comprehensive music education, another reason a competent teacher is necessary.

If, thanks to our music, we make true listening a priority and we develop the ability to listen at a deep level, it will not only improve your piano playing but can enrich the rest of your life in innumerable ways.

One last aspect of personal character I want to touch on as it relates to music and to life is that of HUMOR. Some non-musicians think all classical music is serious, high-brow, no fun and raise their eyebrows in surprise or disbelief when they are told that there is humor in music… and I don't just mean music comedians like Victor Borge, Tom Lehrer, Spike Jones, the Smothers Brothers, Peter

Schickele (P.D.Q. Bach), Anna Russell, Adam Sandler, Allan Sherman, and the list could go on.

No, I mean that there is musical humor in classical music being performed as it was written, as the composer intended. The famous classical period composer Franz Joseph Haydn is especially known for the humor in his music. It is not the knee-slapping variety but rather it's clever, subtle humor that delights the listener. Some of the humor in so-called serious music requires musical knowledge and music listening experience in order to "get it"; it's an inside joke for people in the music-loving community.

As a music student it is a good idea to be alert to the humor in music lest you miss it and rob yourself of some of the pleasure inherent in what you are doing. In addition, it will help you with your practicing and performing if you keep a sense of humor in play. You are doing this for pleasure; so don't make it all so serious that you can't have fun in the midst of your hard work.

The musical skills we have discussed in this Mediant chapter have their corresponding value as personal character traits in the kind of person we are and the kind of life we lead. We can improve our music and ourselves with deliberate practice to develop these skills/traits.

♪ ♪ ♪ ♪ ♪

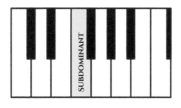

IV

OVERCOMING DISAPPOINTMENT, SETBACKS, DISCOURAGEMENT

Music, Our Friend – Psychological Practicing

Chapter Four, the fourth degree of the scale is the Subdominant. The chord built on the fourth note of the scale, is known as the IV chord or the Subdominant chord and one of its uses is in a cadence (ending) called Plagal. A Plagal cadence is the IV chord going to the I/Tonic chord and its nickname is the "Amen" cadence because it is the ending for church hymns. Anytime you sing an "Amen" at the end of a church hymn, you are hearing a IV–I Plagal Cadence.

So it seemed appropriate for this to be the place we talk about the ways you can use your music to help deal with the sad times, the uncertain times, the devastating times in your life, since church is associated with a place people go to get comfort and guidance when dealing with issues that are confronting them in their lives, and because familiar church hymns often provide such comfort and assurance reinforced by the "so be it" confirmation of "Amen" at the end.

I encourage all of my students, young and old alike, to think of their piano as a special kind of friend. Your piano and the music you make, is a friend for life – a friend that sustains, encourages, challenges, forgives, grows and changes with you, expects your best, responds to your love, is always there waiting for you, gives back more the more you give to it, and it will never leave you.

I like to think of practicing as spending time with that friend. The more time you spend together, the better friends you become. You share your daily ups and downs; sitting on your piano bench, you can laugh, cry, scream, whatever you are feeling. You know that a friend that you see or talk to everyday is a more comfortable, deeper friend than someone you only correspond with once a year just to keep in touch. And as with any friend there will be times when you may be a bit at odds with each other, but you make up and things are good again. A longtime friend like that is who you turn to when you are feeling down, confused, discouraged or when you have suffered a major loss or been given some very bad news.

Music can invigorate, revive, restore – even when sleep can't. Music comforts, reassures, restores Hope. Music heals, even when nothing else can. (There is a lot of research available now testifying to the ways music is being used to heal.)

Use good psychology with your practicing and what you do with your time at the piano. Just like you would share your feelings with your best friend and let them know how they can help, open up at your piano and welcome what it will give you. Use your music to relieve stress and anxiety, to help you cope with problems, to combat depression or loneliness, whatever you need. Decide what it is that you need and then play the pieces or the exercises that will provide that.

For instance, sometimes what will help the most is drilling some technic; routine and repetition can distract us from whatever thoughts are disturbing us. Other times we may need to cry, and playing a tender, sad, emotionally wrenching piece may provide the catharsis we need. If you are just feeling a bit lethargic and need a shot of energy, try playing some ragtime; it's hard to stay blue when that "ragged time" grabs us.

Your Music is a Gift:
from you,
from those who love and encourage you,
from your music mentors,
from composers and musicians thru time,
from the Universe.
Accept all it has to give you!
It will sustain you
and enrich your life.

♪ ♪ ♪ ♪ ♪

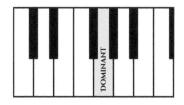

V

CREATIVITY AND FREEDOM

Freedom – Structure, Discipline, Technic –
Improvisation – Rubato

Dominant is the name of the fifth note in the scale and it is the most important position after number I, the Tonic. It is the place you most often can be found if you are not at home. The Tonic and Dominant are close relatives, best friends, president and vice-president, co-captains of the team, Johnny Carson and Ed McMahon (if you are old enough to remember "Heeeeeeeeeere's Johnny!")

The Dominant is like a trumpet fanfare announcing the arrival of the King or Queen, like a spotlight shining on the star walking on stage, like the second to your motion, like the concert master tuning the orchestra awaiting the arrival of the conductor.

A Perfect/Full Cadence, the V to the I, is the most common way to end a section of a piece or the entire piece. It is satisfying to the listener, sounds like things are as they should be. The Dominant (V) points to the Tonic (I)...like hearing a siren and then seeing the emergency vehicle, or seeing and smelling a favorite food and anticipating the taste before we take a bite. We are used to one preceding the other.

On the other hand, if the order of the notes/chords is reversed I to V, everything is left up in the air. That is music's equivalent of asking a question, a question mark. For example, if you are watching a two-part mystery, the music at the end of part one is likely to end with that I-V Half Cadence to leave you hanging, uncertain as to what is going to happen in part two. Ending a phrase or a composition on V leaves things open; one can imagine a number of aural alternatives that might be coming.

So we will use this scale degree to talk a bit about Creativity and Freedom, so necessary in music, and the complement to the stability of the Tonic/Home. Without creativity and freedom our music sounds robotic, emotionless. However, with unbounded freedom music can sound chaotic, unintelligible, confusing, and may just fall apart.

As with much of the world's greatest creative achievements (in music, art, inventions, etc,), we see how the freedom that made the work what it is grew out of Structure/

Discipline. Structure and discipline are the basis for real FREEDOM and Creativity, not the opposite of it. Here in this chapter I am using the Dominant and the Tonic as symbolic of that close relationship.

It becomes obvious to any aspiring pianist that we practice technic – scales, cadences, arpeggios, double thirds, octaves, trills, etudes; Hanon, Czerny, Burmuller, Heller, MIKROKOSMOS, Dohnanyi, Pischna, Cramer – to be able to play our music concentrating on what will make it beautiful and inspiring and not on simply trying to get the notes and all the basics correct. If our technic is easy, smooth, flawless, we have the freedom to be creative, to be musical, to enjoy what we are playing. Technic is the means to the end, NOT the end.

We want to be able to let go and fly, explore, dream, delight in our music. Music encourages us to think outside the box, to try something new! A new piece, a new style of music, a new solution to a technical problem, a new way of seeing ourselves, a new and expanded view of the world. Maybe that spirit can be transported into some other aspects of your life as well. But wherever you encounter it, it will bring you joy and a new sense of Freedom.

One of the music skills you can explore and develop is IMPROVISATION. Improvisation is extemporaneously inventing variations on a melody or on the spot creating

new melodies, rhythms, and harmonies. It is instanta-
neous composing while performing. Again, improvisation depends on technic, knowledge of musical styles, and
experience... and a certain amount of "Courage" (our
Lion over our shoulder).

Improvisation nowadays is most often linked in people's minds with jazz. But the truth is that many of the
great classical composers were in fact master improvisers.
For example, Bach, Mozart, and Beethoven all thrilled
audiences with their spontaneous improvisations. And
musicians in the Baroque era (about 1600–1750) would
entertain themselves by having one person improvise a
melody and then all the others see how many variations
they could improvise on that theme (their equivalent of
video games?!).

I remember reading a book a number of years ago
that talked about our Life as Improvisation. Isn't that
true? Think of the plans you had for your life when you
were 18, 25, 35, 50, 65. How many of them happened
the way you had planned? Life is a constant series of sit-
uations that don't go as planned and require a creative
response.

Improvisation is a necessary life-saving, life-giving
skill. The better you become at improvising, "rolling with
the punches", the happier and less stressful your life is.
We have all known someone who experienced something
traumatic in their life and they were just never able to
"bounce back" from it. But we have also had friends or
known of people who went through things just as bad,

perhaps even worse, and yet they not only lived through it but they used that experience to learn, grow, reassess, to move into a whole new aspect of life. Their "improvisational skills" emerged, or perhaps they had been developed and honed on many smaller life challenges and setbacks along the way.

The attitude that we inculcate by trying our hand at musical improvisation perhaps is the ingredient needed when life circumstances demand our best creative improvisatory response.

When playing music of the Romantic period (roughly 1820–early 1900s) one of the stylistic characteristics to be learned is something called RUBATO. Known by its Italian name, "tempo rubato" literally means "stolen time". The performer makes slight changes in tempo, speeding up slightly and then slowing down within the musical phrase. This expressive rhythmic freedom is what gives the music its emotional pull and power. Anyone who loves Chopin's piano music has fallen prey to his "rubato". And anyone playing Chopin's wonderful music learns the connection between structure and freedom, and works hard to acquire the necessary aural sensitivity to know just how far to stretch the give and take. (This is one of those learnings passed from Master to Apprentice, Teacher to Student. It has to be heard and subtly acquired over time.)

Rubato is another of those musical insights that can have bearing on living. Think about how important it is to be flexible and to know when to be flexible and when not to. Think of poor Tevye in FIDDLER ON THE ROOF and the way he wrestled with the requests of his daughters. With each one he was being asked, pleaded with, required, to bend and stretch his centuries-old religious beliefs even more. He needed to figure out where the limits were. When do we need to hold firm, keep the tempo absolutely steady? And when is it much better to relax, let go a bit, be flexible? And if the latter, how far? This is rubato applied to life.

Just as in music, rubato works best when it is in response to a steady beat (more of that freedom within structure stuff). If done at the right time and in the right amount, appropriate to the piece and the style, then it is absolutely gorgeous and 'speaks' in an emotionally moving and effective way. Applying that kind of 'rubato' in life can turn something boring into something meaningful and beautiful. It might even transform a tense moment into one of relief, or move a would-be adversary into becoming a potential friend. But it always, in music and in life, requires discretion and sensitivity and listening to your inner voice.

The Dominant, the complement to the Tonic – Freedom and the Security of Home and Structure – V and I dependent on each other… Music is dependability, expectability, security, comfort mixed with soaring and freedom. Music lifts us out of the trivia of everyday. Music lifts us out of our geographical place, our place in time, the details of our body and color of our skin. Music is grounded Freedom. As a young student of mine said at his lesson one day, "When I play music, I feel like I'm home even if I'm not."

♪ ♪ ♪ ♪ ♪

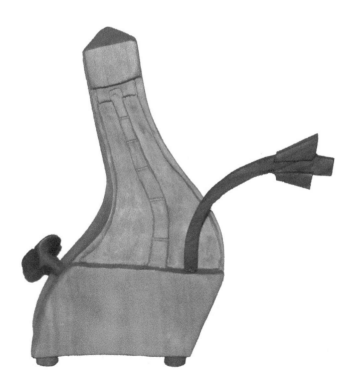

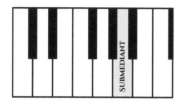

VI

COMMUNICATION

Expression – Interpretative Function – Control –
Remembering – Thinking – Self-Identity –
Communicating with Others – Creative Activity,
Freedom – Risk in Communication –
Body Language – Articulations (Touch Types) –
Silence – Deceptive Cadence

Communication is what music is about; it is a language. One definition of language: "Language is a system of communication used by a particular country or community". In this case, a language used by the human species; music is a universal language. In an article featured by PsychologyDiscussion.net seven functions of language were outlined. I have used their function headings but have applied them to talk about Music as a Language.

Function #1. Expressive and Communicative Functions:

Music is often referred to as "the language of our emotions". Music allows us to express every human emotion and even more than one at the same time. Often it surpasses what is able to be said in words. I would argue that music is a superior form of communication and one that all people should use, as Dr. Suzuki advocated.

Function #2. Interpretative Functions:

Music can certainly help us to interpret and make sense of our world and our feelings. We can be a tangle of matted strings in our brain, and music can help untangle it. If our mind and/or emotions are chaotic and we are muddled, then listening to, or better yet playing a favorite piece of music can calm us down and help us see clearly what it is that is before us or in us.

Function #3. Control Functions:

Music used in its less desirable forms, such as to convince a consumer to buy a certain product or a citizen to rally around a particular cause, certainly seeks to control and manipulate people. But pure (let's even call it 'organic') music doesn't want to control people but rather to move them to feel, to imagine, to experience, to envision, to dream, to connect.

**Function #4. The Functions of Remembering
and Thinking:**

Music is one of the most powerful tools for remembering. It is like an aural photo album or journal, bringing back entire pictures in our heads with all of the accompanying emotions that we were feeling at the time. Sometimes those are memories that we didn't even know we had until the familiar music all at once presented them to us. It is well documented that music unlocks forgotten memories and abilities in people suffering from brain injuries or dementia. But it is true for all of us. Music retrieves precious memories for us.

As a musician, one of the delights we experience is playing a piece that has been a 'close friend' for years which contains multiple levels of memories and meaning. A piece can even serve as a measuring stick like the penciled height marks on the door casing in your childhood home, marking every time you grew another inch. As we play, we remember when certain technical skills were challenging or when we didn't yet have the musical maturity to really understand what a certain passage was 'saying'. Or the piece can bring back a series of different times in our lives and what our hopes and goals and worldview were at the time.

As for thinking, there are many scientific studies and books written which show how regularly engaging in music as a player improves brain function. The information is quite impressive and makes its own case for why adults should seriously consider choosing music as an avocation. (Such research is not going to be included here, but I would encourage you to avail yourself of it.)

Function #5. The Discovery of One's Name: Formation of Self-Concept and Self-Identity:

Primarily it is our self we are communicating with when we make music. We are discovering who we really are, inside – not who the world thinks we are, but who we truly are deep down! We are getting in touch with feelings that sometimes we didn't realize we had or didn't understand how deeply we felt them. We are learning it is good to express them; music gives us an acceptable (even beautiful) way to do that. We may see that there are many more things to like and admire in ourselves than we realized.

This is not bragging; this is the healthy self-love spoken of in the Golden Rule when we are told to "love your neighbor as yourself". The wisdom of psychologists, philosophers, theologians says that we are unable to truly love another if we don't first love ourselves. And we see in the news daily examples of horrible things done by people who sadly lack such healthy self-love. Music gives us time to be with ourselves and to get to know our self intimately, at the same time that we are on an adventure to play music that speaks to us and moves our emotions.

Function #6. Social Functions of Language:

Our goal as a music performer is to communicate heart-to-heart with our fellow human-beings – our family, friends, neighbors, the audience. And it is important to keep focused on that goal. (We will talk more about this in our discussion of Nervousness in the next chapter.)

Music brings people together who may have nothing else in common and allows them to communicate in intimate and meaningful ways. Chamber music can lead to the ultimate in sophisticated cooperation and communication, requiring both verbal and musical conversations that get to the very heart of the music and the musicians. Sharing music allows us to get to know someone at a deep level and often leads to a richer friendship than we perhaps have with someone we have known much longer but not at that level.

Thanks to music I have become friends with people I would never have met and gotten to know, people who have introduced me to cultures, lifestyles, ways of thinking that I never would have known at all or perhaps would have only known by name, in words only, and not in my understanding, in my heart.

My life has been so broadened and enriched not only by music directly but by the people I have met and become friends with through music. What a joy and blessing!

Function #7. Creative Functions:
Music uses melody, and rhythm, and harmony, and tone, and dynamics, and types of touch, and silence, and body language. It has so very many ways to communicate our thoughts and feelings, our wishes and dreams.

Nothing allows such an opportunity to break free and use our creative imagination as does music. Sometimes it teams up with words, but it doesn't have to have words. We pianists can say everything we want to say without the use of words. Talk about FREEDOM! We are freed from words which can limit, derail, confuse, keep our spirit from soaring.

Although I myself love words and really appreciate the use of well-chosen, well executed words, I honestly believe that as a current society the U.S. often places too much value on words to the exclusion of other means of communication. Sometimes things can be expressed better in other ways, especially when emotions play a crucial role. Being comfortable in non-verbal ways of communicating gives a person a much larger "vocabulary" for living.

One personal example, several years ago when my family and I were attending a dear friend's wedding in Nepal, I went on many little excursions out from the hotel on my own. I did not speak the language and am embarrassed to say I knew almost nothing about the country before our trip other than what our friend had told us. But I met wonderful, friendly people and had delightful 'conversations' and even visits to a couple of homes, thanks to their sparse English and my willingness to use Kinesics (popularly known as "body language"). The reason I was comfortable doing that, in spite of looking pretty silly I'm sure, is because I don't think of words as my only possibility of communicating. Being freed of a total dependence on words requires giving up a necessity of feeling in control, not focusing on your appearance (your ego), and yes, at least a bit of "Courage".

Indeed any communication – whether through words, music, body language, dance, other arts – requires some degree of RISK: the risk of being misunderstood, the risk of appearing ignorant or amateurish or (fill in your own blank), the risk of not being taken seriously, the risk of turning off people you care about, the risk of doing damage to your own self-image. So we often feel a need to call on our friend "Courage".

BODY LANGUAGE and ARTICULATIONS:

Picking up on the Body Language mentioned above, I want to talk more specifically about how Body Language applies to playing the piano. Let's examine the Kinesics of approaching the piano, sitting at the piano and playing, and leaving the piano.

How you walk to the piano already gives a message about how you feel about what you are about to do. If you are walking tall and purposely toward the piano, that gives whoever is listening the idea that what they are going to hear is going to be good because you look confident and eager to share your music with them. If on the other hand, your body is bent and you are looking down and your pace is hesitant, then the listeners are already expecting something less than exhilarating or inspiring.

And at the end of your piece, when people are thanking you (for clapping is simply a non-verbal 'thank you for playing for me/us'), if you don't bow (or at least smile and make some gesture as crossed hands over your heart), then people may think you are so egotistical and wrapped up in yourself that you don't care that they just thanked you; instead you just ignored them. Not acknowledging their applause is not a sign of humility, but the opposite. At least, it says that you have no manners, are ignorant of concert etiquette.

If after your performance when your friends start to clap, you make a sad face and shake your head while mouthing 'no' and making a no gesture with your hands in front of your body, it says to them that they are musically stupid because they liked something that wasn't that good. Again, your disappointment in your playing turns into a double negative: you are unhappy and you are making them unhappy. No matter how many mistakes you made or how lacking in polish and finesse you feel your performance was you should always smile at the audience and graciously bow! (Besides, most likely you have blown up the so-called mistakes and do not have a realistic picture of how you played – more on that later.)

Now let's talk about while you are actually playing, the connection between Body Language and what it communicates, the cause-and-effect nature of every motion we make causing some effect in the SOUND we produce, beginning with where we sit in relation to the piano. We need to sit on the front third to half of the piano bench so that we can easily and quickly move from side to side and forward. We don't settle in on the bench as though it were our favorite easy chair, but rather it is simply a balance point that allows us to be ready for action. (All athletes have a ready position: picture a swimmer, a runner, a tennis player, a baseball batter, a football player in the line, each one ready for the moment the action begins.) And the piano bench needs to be back far enough that we can reach all 88 keys with freedom of motion. That means your arms and legs are forward with a slight bend at the elbow and knee, not at right angles which can produce robotic type motions.

Not only do you get a less-constrained tone and have the potential for a bigger sound, but there is a psychological reason as well to having the bench back farther from the keys than you might have assumed. It is a much more positive feeling to be coming toward something than to be trying to get away from it. (To give a non-musical example, have you ever encountered a person who somehow didn't get socialized to learn body distancing and they talk to you with their nose practically touching yours? You are uncomfortable and keep backing away, and if they continue to close the physical space, you find yourself getting annoyed. And probably the next time you see them coming your way, you may just cross the street or go in at the nearest doorway.)

Now, finally the actual playing…If we want a smooth rolling accompaniment to enhance a lovely legato connected melody, our arm must be moving in a fluid circular unbroken motion with no stops or bumps or snags. On the contrary, if the tune is a lively, snappy invigorating dance, then the type of motion we use to produce that sound must be angular, precise, short with plenty of air holes between the notes. Now I am speaking of articulations, which I prefer to call TOUCH TYPES on the piano (not to be confused with "touch typing" on a typewriter). There are many "touch types" depending on the sophistication of the pianist, but let's 'touch' on just the three most basic ones right now:

ARTICULATED touch type: Each note is separate. You hear the beginning of the note and the end of the note. It is played by a straight down and up motion of the finger.

LEGATO touch type: Notes are smoothly connected on one breath if singing or playing a wind instrument, on one direction of the bow on string instruments. On the piano fingers shift the weight cleanly from one finger to the next. The two keys have to pass each other exactly in the middle; as one key is coming up, the next key is going down. The hand is moving in a smooth horizontal direction in contrast to the vertical direction for Articulated notes.

STACCATO touch type: Notes are short, detached. Technically, a staccato note is half of the length it would be if there were no dot under or over it, and the other half of the note becomes a rest (silence). To get the sharp, crisp sound of a staccato the motion is forward, not vertical as in Articulated or horizontal as in Legato. The finger goes forward toward the backboard of the piano and just dips down long enough to depress the key in its forward trajectory, as a plane that briefly touches ground and keeps going. The forward motion allows the finger to get out of the way so the key can bounce up instantly, doesn't have to wait for the finger to change from a down to up direction. This produces a brittle, crackling sound like stepping on dried autumn leaves. As you can see, the type of motion used (the body language) gets translated into the type of sound that comes out, and the type of sound creates the feelings, the message you want to communicate.

Touch types are like facial expressions and are as crucial in music as are facial expressions when someone is speaking. In the latter, an absence of facial expression is known as "flat affect" and is a sign of some medical issue, i.e. is not the normal condition. To make music "speak" it must be played with the touch type appropriate to any given note. A mistake in a touch type may actually be more serious than if you played a wrong note. Touch types are important tools in our musical toolbox, and they need to be of good quality and sharpened up.

SILENCE:

In a chapter on Communication and the Language of music we MUST delve into SILENCE. Another bare-bones definition of music is "Sound and Silence organized in time to convey a certain message or feeling." Notice that it is the combination of sound and silence! Music is not non-stop sound.

Silence is not a nothing, not just an absence of sound. Silence is something; it has meaning. And there are different kinds of silence with many different meanings, both in music and in life.

One of the most dramatic uses of silence in music is Beethoven's Fifth Symphony. It begins with rests/silence and the theme is characterized by those silences that some have interpreted as fate calling. Suspenseful music makes expert use of well-placed silences. In quiet, meditative music, silences add to the calming effect. Silence can be used to shine a spotlight on something surprising that follows it. When something is awesome, silence is sometimes the most effective way to express that.

To illustrate how silence can have very different meanings, imagine seeing a person sitting alone at a coffee shop. He is just taking a break to reboot before his next business appointment. Being there alone has no particular significance. But what if he has proposed to the love of his life, and she is supposed to meet him there to give him her answer. It is long past the agreed upon meeting time and he is still there by himself. In this case the absence and the silence are the answer, and he is devastated. The silence is heavy.

Sometimes silence is comforting, sometimes scary, sometimes questioning, sometimes motivating...sometimes silence is light and sometimes heavy...sometimes it is expected but sometimes a surprise...sometimes it is solitary and sometimes shared.

In music we learn that silence (rests) is equal in importance to sound (notes). In a far too busy, far too noisy world we would all do well to have more silence. It seems that many people are afraid of silence and surround themselves with sound of some sort all the time, a lot of it being electronic. Constant noise steals thinking time, creativity, inner calm, and possibly even one's health. If music can teach a person to appreciate, even crave, the quiet times, Silence, then that is another profound gift for which to thank our dear friend Music.

Now that we have been discussing music as a language, as communication, you are probably wondering how that connects with the sixth step of the musical scale known as the Submediant. In a music theory text, you are apt to find an explanation something like this: "The submediant (vi) chord functions as a weak pre-dominant. Its most typical role is leading from the tonic to a strong pre-dominant (such as IV or ii). The common tones between the submediant and all of these chords **allow for *smooth and easy*** *voice-leading.*" Now it is not my purpose to get into all of that right now and perhaps even scare you away from your desire to play the piano. So I will just call your attention to the words in bold. This chord is allowing for smooth passage from one chord to another leading to important closing cadences. It is lubricating passages, facilitating communication.

Another role the Submediant chord plays is in its own cadence known as a Deceptive Cadence. That is a V chord (the Dominant) that goes unexpectedly to the vi chord instead of back to the I chord (Tonic) as our ears are anticipating. When we think we are going home, we all at once end up somewhere else (on the sixth degree of the scale). Not only that, but if we are in a Major key (as was discussed in Chapter 3), we are taken to a **minor** sound instead of the Major we were counting on. So it is a double shock, a real surprise. And that automatically extends the length of the piece because the piece cannot stop there; it HAS to get to home. So there is additional material added to bring us around again to where we can actually land on HOME – much like an airplane that comes in as though to land but then has to circle around and try again, this time landing in the designated spot, and everyone gives a satisfied deep sigh and smiles.

While we are talking about Deceptive Cadences, let's look at a possible application to life. How many times do we encounter Detours in our lives: in our jobs, in our family life, in our goals? And we need to invest more time and effort into figuring out how to get back home, how to get back on track, on the road that will lead us to where our gut tells us we want or need to be. Deceptive Cadences, whether in music or life, are a surprise and have a purpose; they are not bad (as the word itself might imply). They can add to our delight and make our final arrival at home even sweeter.

♪ ♪ ♪ ♪ ♪

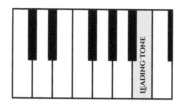

VII

LIFE

Keeping Going – Dissonances – Little Things –
Perfection – Authenticity – "Enough" –
Guilt – Breathing – Nervousness (Psychology,
Practicing Performing) – Role Model – Fear –
Artistic Power – Diminished Chord – Unity/
Community – Passion – Well-Balanced

The penultimate degree of our Major scale, the seventh note, is called the Leading Tone because it is just half a step below the octave, the end note of the scale. It is so close that we feel if we just reached a teeny bit more, we would be at the finish line. So this chapter is designated LIFE – the challenges, the learnings, the rewards.

We have already spoken about the importance and necessity of Keeping Going: playing one note after the other, putting one foot in front of the other NO MATTER WHAT and of "improvising", being creative when something unexpected happens to try to stop that forward progression.

Music, like Life, has its DISSONANT SOUNDS, its ugly, challenging times and that is often what moves the music, and us, forward. If we can learn to grow from those discordant sounds and not live in dread of them, then we can enjoy the total composition.

We experience repeatedly in music how LITTLE THINGS MATTER, how they can make a huge difference. Taking time to get a fingering, touch type, dynamic level, phrase marking just right can make all the difference, and a piece which was just an assemblage of notes all at once becomes a beautiful work of art, an inspiration.

How many times in life is it the surprise visit, a needed hug, a thoughtful note, a helpful errand, an arm on the shoulder, a word of encouragement that makes a huge difference to you and is never forgotten? Good intentions are not enough in playing the piano or in living our life. It is the follow-through that counts: taking the time, being thoughtful, listening, empathizing.

In talking about being in the space of the Leading Tone and reaching for the top, it is necessary to consider the concept of PERFECTION. Is Perfection your goal in Music, in Life? What do you mean by perfection? If you mean by that absolutely no flaws or imperfections, then surely we would all have to admit that that is not possible, not an achievable goal. Even the dictionary definition says: "the condition, state, or quality of being free **or as free as possible** from all flaws or defects; the action or process of improving something until it is faultless **or as faultless as possible**". The vision (an aural vision in music) of perfection is important, but we must realize that though we might continually be moving toward it, we will never achieve it and we must not disparage ourselves or get discouraged or worse yet give up because of that.

We might even consider another goal, that of AUTHENTICITY. Look at these synonyms for "Authenticity": Genuineness, Originality, Rightfulness, Legitimacy, Validity, Reliability, Dependability, Trustworthiness, Truth, Faithfulness, Fidelity, Credibility, Accuracy. Being authentic with the music, being authentically ourselves and communicating authentically, living authentically. Perhaps you will want to consider that as a goal that is within a human being's reach.

Related to what we are talking about is a concept that is crucial in music and also has serious implications for living. The musical word is INTONATION. Everyone understands what that means; it means accuracy of pitch in playing or singing. When referring to an instrument, it means tuning the instrument to the proper pitch (generally 'A' at 440) and then playing the notes in tune. In addition to playing the piano, I also have the extreme pleasure of owning and playing a harpsichord, which being truly a string instrument needs tuning every time it is played. So I had to learn how to tune it. But I am not a professional tuner and am slow at it, giving me a lot of time to reflect on what I am doing. Some of that reflection has been about the very nature of tuning, that it is turning the string just the right amount – not too much and not too little. The aim is to arrive at "Enough".

That idea of "ENOUGH" has aroused all kinds of thoughts in my being. What if instead of always wanting more of _____ (fill in the blank with whatever applies to you), you decided you would try to determine what would constitute "enough" and make that your goal and when you achieved it, arrived there, you would be pleased, satisfied, even happy? Being in tune is a prerequisite for beautiful music. And isn't being in tune in life going to produce a beautiful outcome as well?

Using these intentions of "Authenticity" and "Enough" to counter some of the negative consequences of striving for "Perfection" can help us tremendously psychologically while still inspiring and encouraging us to go for the best we can be. We must break the habit of assuming something awful is going to happen if we don't do a task perfectly. Putting that kind of stress on ourselves can rob us of the Joy we are meant to experience.

That leads right into another negative we need to rid ourselves of as aspiring pianists, as adult piano students, and that is GUILT. That is a "habit" that can be acquired, or often accepted as a 'gift' from family members, coworkers or a boss, even so-called friends. I tell my piano students when they enter my studio that they are entering a NO-GUILT ZONE. Because an adult has decided to spend their time and money and effort learning to play the piano, they feel they must make good on that expenditure and can very easily feel guilty if it doesn't seem to them that they are measuring up, learning as fast as they should or as many pieces as another student. (Of course, it doesn't help if a spouse for instance points out that they are not practicing enough to make their investment of family money and time worth it.)

It always makes me sad if a student comes in apologizing for the fact that they have not had much time for piano practice that week. I tell them I know they did the best they could do to juggle everything in their schedule to fit in piano and that I do not in any way take that personally. I tell them that I understand that they wish they had more time to devote to their practicing and not to feel guilty over it. Guilt just deprives us of the pleasure we can get from our work at the piano. And if the guilt piles up, it can even force us to quit something that we really wanted to do and could have benefitted from. Playing the piano ought to lead to enhancing a person's life, reducing stress, providing pleasure and well-being. In other words,

I want piano to be part of the solution and not part of the problem in people's busy, hectic, stressful lives.

One simple but profound skill and reminder that music provides us is BREATHING. Yes, breathing. It is obvious that a singer and anyone playing a wind instrument has to work a lot on how to breathe to get the maximum amount of air and how to use that air supply efficiently. But we pianists need to use our breath as well! Not only do we need deep breathing to supply our brain with the oxygen needed for all that heavy mental work going on and to provide the power we need throughout our body to play the piano well, but we also use breathing to construct musical phrases that make the message of the music intelligible.

If someone started reading something to you and just kept saying words until they ran out of air and then gasped a breath and kept going, paying no attention to the commas and sentences and paragraphs, you would understand little or none of what they were reading. It is the same with music. If we don't play the "punctuation" in music, it too is nonsensical and anyone listening tunes out – even maybe we ourselves.

So in life, as in our music, we must live/play with meaning, breathing deeply and in the right places. And reminding ourselves to just keep breathing steadily is calming, no matter the activity we are involved in. It is good to take several deep breaths before we begin playing the piano and to have moments of deep breathing throughout our day. Ultimately, it is all about our breath, isn't it?

That segues nicely into the topic of NERVOUSNESS and PERFORMANCE ANXIETY because when we are nervous our breathing reverts to shallow, little breaths that don't give us the air we need and add to the panic we are experiencing.

First, let me say that nervousness in itself is not a bad thing. It shows that we care about what we are doing. If we didn't care or were lackadaisical, we wouldn't be nervous. Nervousness is only bad if, and to the extent, it prevents us from doing our best – from communicating with our music what we want to share with our listeners. Nervousness is not a sign of weakness or cowardice; it is something that needs to be managed. That is done through psychology (the way we think) and plenty of practice, that is Performing.

Let's talk about the psychology involved. When you are performing, you need to switch your focus, your primary concern, away from yourself and your ego to the music and allow it to "speak", to engage and move the listeners. This is not about You and what people are thinking about You, how they are judging You. It is about the communication going on between you and the music and your friends (the "audience"). While you are playing you **must** keep focused on that and **not** on what someone in

the audience is thinking about you! If they are emotionally
involved in the piece as is our goal, they are not thinking about you at all. That only happens if the performer
calls attention to a mistake by pausing, stopping, making
a face, shaking their head, or uttering something. Then
the spell of the music has been broken and the listener has
to be brought back in.

Another thing we can do to control or overcome nervousness is to ask ourselves what is the worst thing that
could happen if we don't play everything 'perfectly'. This
is not our job; so we aren't going to lose our job, our
source of income, our ability to put food on the table.
Our spouse is not going to ask for a divorce. Our friends
are not going to dump us. It is not going to trigger an
IRS audit. Our car is not going to be repossessed. Our
dog is not going to ignore us and stop having anything
to do with us. We will not be boycotted from serving
on a community board because our reputation has been
discredited. Go on…. Think of as many horrible things
as you can until the ridiculousness of it gets through to
you and you start laughing, realizing how overblown and
unfounded your fears are.

Let's face it. The worst thing that can happen is that
you would disappoint yourself, but even that needs to be
looked at in a broader, more comprehensive way. One of
the things I insist on when one of my students is critiqu-
ing him/herself is that they begin by telling me all the
things they did well and things they liked about their per-

formance. Because what happens is that people tend to just recount the mistakes, the mess-ups. I repeatedly have to remind them to LISTEN, really Listen, to their playing, ALL of it. (I have even been known to ask a piano student to count the total number of notes in their piece to point out that missing one or even several out of that huge number is not something to obsess over.) We don't want to be like some journalists or newscasters who only look for the 'bad' stuff! We have to train ourselves to listen to the Tone, the Musicality, the Sensitivity, the story being told – the good stuff. After all, it is the things we did well that we want to reinforce, keep doing. How can we do that if we didn't even hear it. Listen to it all, the big picture!

Perhaps you unfortunately had a parent or aunt or sibling who only criticized and never praised. If you made a 98 on a test, why wasn't it a 100; if you were elected vice-president of the high school student council, why wasn't it president? You completed a 26-mile marathon, well why didn't you win it? We all have encountered that kind of negativity somewhere and it can easily seep into us. Maybe we don't do that to someone else and yet we do it to ourselves. (Think about that self-love we talked about earlier.) Be a friend to yourself, whether in your daily life or in your music performing.

We've looked at how adjusting our thinking can reduce our nervousness and put it in a position where it does no damage. Now we need to acknowledge that the other necessary component is practice – not just our every-day piano practice which is certainly necessary but also "PRACTICE PERFORMING" and actually performing every chance we get.

The daily practice is self-explanatory and obvious. If you have not prepared well, then there is a valid reason to be nervous and there is nothing to say except that perhaps you could have practiced more and practiced better (remember the "**Perfect** practice makes perfect!"). But a pianist can spend the necessary time practicing and doing it the right way and that is still no guarantee that their performance will go as they would like.

"Performing" is an additional piano skill to be learned, practiced. The minute you add even one person in the room with you and your piano, the whole experience feels different even if that person is your spouse, your child, your best friend, or your piano teacher – all people you know who are on your side, rooting for you, cheering you on. But the communication circle has expanded, and you need to gain experience in this new environment.

I work with my students in depth on how to "PRACTICE PERFORMING". Set a specific day (tomorrow) and time (7 p.m.) when you are going to "perform" your piece. That means you will come to the piano cold (i.e., not in the middle of your regular practice session), bow, sit down at the piano, prepare your head and ears and hands, play your piece from first note to last note with NO un-notated Stops, Pauses, Hesitancies, "stutters" (on-the-spot corrections). "End" the piece with finesse, stand up with a smile and bow (there Has to be applause), and exit (walk away from the piano). Doing that, even with no one listening, gives us a small simulation of performing. It is the necessity of keeping going without stopping to fix or improve something and knowing that we have only once chance that makes it scary and brings on nervousness.

As for the audience, it can even be stuffed animals for children. Adults often begin with a recording device as their "audience" and then move to inviting a family member, a neighbor, the mailman... anyone! Just say you have a favor to ask of them and that it will only take three minutes, five minutes (however long your piece is). Explain to them what it is you are doing, that you have been working months to learn this piece and you are going to perform it at _____ in a (week) and that what you need now is to get comfortable playing it for people. When you say it like that, they are happy to be of help and often feel very pleased and honored that you would ask because they understand that this is something very personal and important to you. You are taking a risk sharing your deepest self with them in this special way, and they appreciate that.

The only thing it takes from them is that small amount of time and their **complete attention!** The latter is crucial because you need to know that they are really listening, that your music is not just background while they do something else. In fact, the more formal you can make the situation, the better. We want you to feel nervous so that you get used to playing in that state.

An experienced performer can get to the point where their nervousness kicks in the adrenalin and the result is that we play our piece the best we have ever played it and we are on cloud nine (the musician's alternative to doing drugs). After our frequent practice performing dates (maybe even one a day always designated enough ahead so that we are thinking about it and anticipating it), then set up small performances leading to an ever-expanding audience depending on what your goal is. For instance, you have been asked to play at a community event of some sort. Start with one or two close family members, then a group of several friends, then a dinner party, next at one of your clubs you belong to – gradually building up the total number of people and the number of people you don't know personally.

I belong to professional music teacher organizations that have performing opportunities for adult amateur musicians and those are wonderful events to participate in. But for most of my students performing at our own studio recitals (I call them Piano Parties and they include a potluck meal and plenty of socializing in addition to the piano performances) and playing for their families and friends is the extent of their performing. Or sometimes someone will play at their church.

So to recap, in order to share your music with some-one else – known as "performing", it is necessary to prac-tice sufficiently, to "practice performing", to perform reg-ularly/frequently, AND to do the important "head work" we talked about. If you do all of this, then you will be able to enjoy performing. Performing should not be something to dread and just make it through.

Now to apply all this to your Life: think about the way you critique yourself in other parts of your life and apply the same kind of criteria of looking at the big picture and seeing all the good while taking note of the things that could use a bit of improvement or redirection. Be sure to acknowledge the good stuff! Clap for yourself, pat yourself on the shoulder, say "Good job!" (just as I have my stu-dents do every time they accomplish some minor task they are practicing). Of course, extend that kind of enthusiasm and praise to others when they are tackling something new and challenging.

Let me say here that as an adult piano student, espe-cially a Beginner, you are a ROLE MODEL and an inspi-ration for others. You may have a friend who has always wanted to play the flute, or oil paint, or do pottery and now they see that it is possible to take up a brand-new exciting adventure like that, even as a middle aged or senior adult. And you may have a grandchild that stores that picture away and in later years may decide to learn to play the piano (or follow some other dream) because they remember you did that and really liked it.

When you become comfortable performing at the piano, that often gets transferred to other areas as well. I have had students say that before their life and experience as an amateur pianist that they would never get up and speak at a meeting or large gathering of any kind, but now it is no big deal. They are comfortable running a meeting, making a presentation, speaking on behalf of a cause they believe in, taking part in a worship service, etc. Frequency doing anything makes that activity more comfortable, whatever it is. We are erecting good habits in our lives.

In all areas of our life, I would suggest that we are most effective, most appreciated, better loved if our focus is on the other person, the task at hand, the goal and not on building up our own ego. Being authentic and exhibiting integrity is always a big plus and goes a long way in getting people on our team. Taking the risk to communicate clearly and honestly and from the heart is as important in life as in sharing our music. How many of the world's problems could be eradicated or at least lessened by deep heart-to-heart, soul-to-soul connections, one person to another?!

Fear stifles, blocks, pulls down, paralyzes, discredits, robs. We must use will power and right thinking to overcome our Fear! Fear can prevent us from taking emotional risks, but playing it safe doesn't allow us to reach the heights to which we aspire. With our friend "Courage" in our pocket, we bravely step forward to do difficult, scary things knowing that we will grow and become stronger and will have the opportunity to experience the riches of living.

We have not spoken of POWER and that is certainly a prevalent aspect of life in the real world. Consider how much of the news we are bombarded with daily is about power of one sort or another: Military power, Political power, Economic power, Social power, Religious power – power of one group over another, power of one person over another or many others – and so it goes. "Sheer physical strength or the ability to control someone else or the situation to benefit oneself or group" – the most widely used definition of power – does not impress me and is not a goal I have ever claimed for myself.

But I want to mention the kind of power I do aspire to: "ARTISTIC POWER", the ability to produce the desired effect, to intellectually and emotionally "move" the person or persons on the other end of our musical connection. For me "Artistic Power" is akin to "Moral Power" in the non-music areas of life. Both seek to create something beautiful and meaningful that brings people together on equal ground. It is not power over another, but rather the power that the two have together to experience beauty and a shared 'truth'.

All of the great composers whose names are common household words exhibit great artistic power in their music and for that to be communicated to living, breathing people in this time and place requires at least a certain degree of artistic power on the part of the current performer. When that happens, the result can be sheer ecstasy which we will say more about in the final chapter.

Everyone has a name come to mind in the realm of Moral Power, a person famous or not who has lived their life with such integrity and concern for the other that their deeds and words inspired us or a whole nation of people to follow their example. Some of the famous names mentioned would surely include: Martin Luther King, Jr., the Dalai Lama, Mother Teresa, Jesus of Nazareth, Moses, Sojourner Truth, Rosa Parks, Buddha...fortunately there are many who could be included in this list. And you hopefully have a person in your life you would include in your own list, someone whose moral power has influenced you and the decisions you make.

Interestingly, I would like to point out that unlike people in the earlier Power categories, people who have the greatest artistic power and moral power are frequently people who are characterized by modesty and Humility. They are serving a higher vision or calling and are not out to promote themselves for fame or fortune. They may end up the beneficiaries of those byproducts but that is not their primary goal. A Life Lesson?

Let's talk a bit here about the chord that occurs on this seventh degree of the scale because it is very special and fits with what we have just been talking about. The vii chord is the only one of its kind in a major key. The distance between the three notes of the chord is small (two consecutive minor thirds) and the chord sounds like it has been shrunk, pulled in. Its name is "diminished". It sounds introverted, like a person curled up in a ball trying to hide. People describe the sound as dark, tense, foreboding, even scary. In movies in a dramatic scene in a mystery or in a chase, the background music is apt to have an abundance of diminished chords to add to the suspense. Often there is no dialogue; the music alone creates the mood. But when the vii chord is not particularly frightening, it is at least attention-getting. It needs you to take notice, perhaps like a child who is very sensitive and needs extra care or a person who is grieving and needs TLC. It stands out if you are listening, paying attention.

To play right through a diminished chord as though things were normal or rosy, is akin to committing a crime. You have missed the whole point. If you saw someone sitting in a corner all alone crying, you would need to respond with extra care and thoughtfulness and kindness.

There are many things that could be said here about how this can be applied to living. How many times do we just rush past and not take note of a person or a situation in need of extra care, some kind attention or action from us? In our aspiring to reach the top we must not be so busy or so focused on where we are heading that we miss the meaning, the opportunities to help, that are right there as part of our journey.

Following on this, is the knowledge, belief, that UNITY, COMMUNITY, is important. As a musician we are well aware that each of our body parts has a role to play in our playing a piece of music: every finger, both hands, wrists, arms, feet, back, eyes, ears, lungs, brain... And if you are making music in an ensemble, small or large, every person has their important job to perform. It is not a competition; all are winners. A symphonic orchestra is beautiful to see as well as to hear. What an example of people coming together to create a community with a unified goal and working together to achieve it! Music is certainly a model for how things ought to work in the world. World Peace could be symbolized by one giant orchestra and chorus playing and singing their hearts out and the result being of heavenly proportions.

"Playing their hearts out" means playing with PASSION. Music – and Life – without Passion is a disaster, a "sin", a crime, a waste, a thrown-away opportunity, a shame, a grey world lacking color, a rejection, an insult, [wow, can you tell my button was pressed?]! No need to say any more.

Many people's lives are out of balance. What I mean by that is that not every aspect of them is being utilized. For example, someone who spends the majority of their waking hours doing a job that primarily uses their brain has little or no time for the physical or artistic parts of themselves. On the contrary, an athlete may never make time to take an academic class or engage in a creative activity. It is easy to fill our days with what we have been trained to do or are in a habit of doing. Often that is something we already feel competent at.

Likewise, it is easy to surround ourselves with people doing similar things. Consequently, the activities of our life can become very circumscribed. In that kind of restricted environment there are many different kinds of people, ideas, and activities that we know little or nothing about. Society divided up into groups of people who think and act alike is not healthy for the individuals nor for the society.

Music by its very nature seeks to balance a person, round them out. Whatever is missing or weak has to be developed. To play music well:

> ➤ clear thinking and a high level of brain work is necessary

> ➤ expressing emotion is absolutely essential; there is no music without it

> being systematic, having a plan, and utilizing good study habits are essential

> muscle strength, flexibility, and the highest level of coordination require a special kind of 'athleticism'

> following instructions while also being creative involves discernment and good artistic instincts

> collaborating with peers brings into play social skills

In other words, making music well develops our PHYSICAL, MENTAL, EMOTIONAL, and SPIRITUAL natures and abilities to an extent that possibly nothing else can!

Music expands what we hear and what we understand. It is a deep learning experience enlightening us and enriching us in all of the areas just mentioned. Music inspires, invigorates, encourages, humbles, demands the best we can do. It develops humans to their ultimate level. Music sustains, heals, teaches, remembers, brings pleasure, coordinates, unifies, elevates, demands attention and loyalty, creates bridges, expands our spirituality.

This "Leading Tone" in music is Our Life, reaching for the most we can be as we anticipate arriving at the top, while caring for the "diminished chords" along the way! On this life journey we are both a soloist and part of an ensemble, striving to make beautiful music.

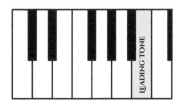

VIII

SPIRITUALITY

Arrival – Spiritual River – Time –
Uni-Directional – Breath of Life – Summary

A RRIVAL AT OUR GOAL: We have reached the final note of our scale, the octave! In music there is such total satisfaction in that arrival. In a piece of music that final Tonic (I) chord brings us Home. Even people who know nothing of music theory understand quite well when they hear this arrival that all has been brought to fruition, that what was intended has been achieved. There is a huge internal sigh, an exhalation of breath, not out of disappointment, or discouragement, or giving up as some sighs might indicate, but rather the deep sigh of completion, of Peace, of rest.

So this chapter is about Music as a Spiritual river flowing through us and connecting us to that part of each one of us that lies beyond rational explanation.

Listening for and appreciating Silence in Music and in Life attunes us to Eternity. Music calls us to melt into the ONE, the eternal, the (aural) vision; to become part of something larger than us.

With music we experience Time in new ways, both smaller (milliseconds) and larger (eternity). Musicians can perceive time differences in milliseconds; for example, a drummer can detect if a beat is off by a few thousands of a second. A piece of music lasting only minutes in ordinary clock time can go through all of those infinitesimally small units of time and yet contain content, meaning, enough to fill up Eternity.

Music is a source of spiritual vision and inspiration. Music, like God, is both Demanding and Forgiving, both Unyielding and Flexible, both Mentor and Friend. Music should not be bastardized for commercial or political or military purposes! Its purpose and goal are spiritual in nature and are of the eternal world, not the ordinary, mundane, self-seeking everyday world. (Great music that has existed for hundreds of years and continues to move people is proof of that.)

Music symbolizes our Life: it, like we, has a starting point and travels on a unique one-way journey until it arrives at its destination. True music is living; recordings while lovely are not real music. Every live performance is different, unique, like each life, and that performance will never be identically repeated. We cannot go back and change the performance; that's why we want to do our best all along the way as we flow toward the finish.

In our music and in our life we want to look forward with anticipation, hope, and eagerness – not fear or dread. Listening, meditation, deep breathing envelop us in Silence, Peace. For some this state of being might even be given a music-like title "Prayer without Words". Music is breath, the breath of life.

Music is constitutive of LIFE. It is the last thing to go when we are dying. Many articles and books have been written about the way music is being used in Hospice Care, such as this PSYCHOLOGY TODAY blog by Marilyn A. Mendoza Ph.D.:

The Power of Music at the End of Life

Music has become such an integral part of our lives that it is hard to imagine living without it. It is not known how long music has been a part of human existence, but there have been discoveries of ancient musical instruments carved out of bone dating back between 43,000–60,000 years ago. However, it is likely that our voices and hands were the first musical instruments. We have long known that music has the power to enhance our lives and promote physical, emotional and spiritual healing. Music is an important part of our celebrations and transitions in life. Our final transition from this life is also a time when the power of music can be important to provide peace and comfort, not only to the dying but to family members as well. Research into the use of music in hospice and palliative care has consistently found that patients, family, and staff all benefit from the music, and often after only one session. Music has been found to help decrease anxiety, agitation, and pain. It also helps patients to slow and deepen their breath.

Music is the breath of life. Music played at the end of one's life is sometimes played in the same tempo as to match the heart rate; it is perfectly synchronized to match the person's breathing. Music can provide the aural river that gently slides our soul from this existence to the next, from this world to that larger, eternal world.

Sound soars, can go anywhere; it can't be owned and held down. Music reaches beyond our present time and place. It connects us to kindred spirits all around the globe and not just people who are presently here. It allows us to time travel, both backward and forward to faraway times and places. It erases all our walls and boundaries! Through music we connect with people no longer here on the earth in this life while at the same time linking us to generations to come after us. It bridges the great mysterious divide. One can experience a heavenly out-of-body experience while deeply engaged in Music.

Listening to music and especially making our own music expands us; it broadens and deepens our sensitivities, our values, our purpose, our vision. It shares many characteristics with religion without being confined or segregated by dogma. Through sound and silence music makes the all-important indefinable concepts we call Love, Hope, Faith, Prayer, God, Unity, Peace, Beauty, Eternity real to us in the language of our emotions, in the deepest part of our self, our Soul.

Music is a microcosm of Life. Music and Life are both timed entities with a start, a middle, and an end. Time is our creative medium; how we use it, what we do with it, is our work of art. What we make of our Life is our major Creative work, our composition.

Each of us is a theme, a Melody, and our life is a series of Variations on the Theme. When our "song" has ended, will we leave a beautiful unique melody that lingers on to delight and inspire others?

> Make beautiful Music.
> Make a beautiful Life.

♪ ♪ ♪ ♪ ♪

CODA

Just as a Coda sums up and finishes off a piece of music, this is the time when I can give you my last heartfelt 'notes'.

"My wish for you is that your music will make your life richer, more enjoyable, more meaningful, more inspiring, more fulfilling, and more peaceful at the Finale. May the themes of your life reappear triumphantly transformed in a dramatic climax, leaving beautiful music in the hearts of all who love you."

♪ ♪ ♪ ♪ ♪

POSTLUDE

With heartfelt thanks to all my students through a lifetime of teaching piano: adults of all ages and stages, my beloved inmate students, children, and teens. Thanks for trusting me, for sharing your personal journey (music and life) with me, for your "Patience" and "Courage", for your humor, and your Love.

What an honor and a privilege to make music with you and to become deep friends.

With thanks to all who helped make this book for adults aspiring to make their own beautiful music at the piano.

♪ ♪ ♪ ♪ ♪

Just for Fun...

At the end of each of my teaching semesters my adult students have a Piano Party (a recital but with a shared meal and lots of time for socializing). I pick one or two of the most memorable things one of them has said at a lesson and they are presented a parchment certificate with their quote and the date and circumstance of their remark. It adds to the fun of the event. Following are quotes that have appeared on these certificates given to my adult piano students through the years.

Encore

*Quotes from Adult Piano Students
during their Private Lessons*

"Don't get ideas in your head about what you're going to hear, preconceived notions of what this piece is going to sound like."

"If I'm going to count calories all week, I'm not going to count with the metronome too!"

On duet-playing:
"At least when two are playing, some of the notes are right!"

Piano teacher: "What is rhythm?"
Piano student: "Something I ain't got."

Teacher: "I want to hear the 3 against 2 measure."
Student: "I bet you do!"

"It was no problem getting here early for the piano lesson,
I quit my job."

"It's different when I'm with Marsha. At home I think I'm
a wonderful pianist. Then I get to my lesson and…"

"It's the PIANO – it's <u>not</u> ME! My piano is so easy; it
just flows. This piano you have to push the keys down!"

My piano student was practicing her Beethoven "Pathetique
Sonata" and then put on a recording of Rubinstein playing
it. Her husband rushed in saying, "Boy, did you get better!" When she played it again, she yelled to him: "I bet
you thought that was Rubinstein!"

"I was so excited with my new metronome that I didn't
get to <u>this</u> piece."

"I don't seem to play well here. I really did play it better
before I came!"

"I'm finding new ways to be wrong."

"Since I've been playing the 1st movement, my hands
have grown older."

"I was doin' so good doin' it wrong!"

"I can play it at 60…I can play it at 120…I can play it at a thousand! It's something about being here! I'm going to quit piano!"

"You know I gave my granddaughter my metronome – good grandma!"

"Don't say 'ah!' You mess me up."

On putting on her glasses:
"Well, it doesn't mean I can play it any better, but at least I can see it."

"Hmmm… I do things here I don't do at home."

"If I don't correct it, you go 'Oops!' And if I do correct it, you say 'Go back and keep going!'"

"You found that mistake once before and I think I corrected it for a day."

"Okay, let's see how I can mangle this today."

"I was miserable anyway, so why not come to piano?!"

"I need some help with notes so I don't hate it [this piece]"

"When I practice it at home, it's fine. I only screw it up here!"

On being an adult beginning piano student:
"You have to realize you're an idiot and just go with it."

On working to play a difficult run in a Chopin nocturne:
"Either the Left hand or the Right hand. I can't do both – your choice. But those right hand notes are so gorgeous they should be on their own!"

"Don't look at me like that – it throws me off!"

On being made to play a section of her piece with the metronome, repeatedly:
"Don't I have to go home now? I'm pretty sure I have to go home now!"

"How long have you been playing? You've been playing longer than I have, right?"

"I like my way better! This is painful! Can I go wash some windows?!"

"I don't want to play it again! I just want to go home!" ("I can't believe I pay for this abuse!")

"I don't look at my piano lesson notebook. It's bad for my health."

"I was doing just fine until you started writing everything down! Now you're stressing me out!"

re: Chopin "Waltz in b":
"If Rubinstein didn't do that little trill in the recording, then I don't have to do it!"

"Do the left-hand chords?! Really?!"

"What time is it? Isn't it time for my lesson to be over?"

Piano teacher: "It worked that time. Can you do it again?"
Piano student: "ooh!"

Student referring to the practice 'Dot Spots' mentioned in chapter II, p. 21:
"NO! Not a dot! A dot is a mark of humiliation."

Piano teacher on the arpeggios in "Autumn Leaves":
"What's happening with the left hand there?"
Piano student: "not much, nothing good"

Piano teacher: "I'm not going to be timing; I'll just be listening."
Piano student: "Oh, don't do that!"

"Any song is an equal opportunity for a meltdown."

"Don't go be tellin' me what to do!"

"If I do shaping, I can't do rhythm."

"I'm going to try to shave off the sides of my fingers so they fit better."

Piano teacher: "Your counting isn't continuous."
Piano student: "No, but I'm playing the right note on the right number – the numbers just aren't at the right time."

Discussing the sound at a piano lesson on Zoom:
"You don't need an upgrade in sound equipment to know what a bad pianist I am."

Piano teacher: "Have you worked on exercise #11?"
Piano student: "Yes, and I have managed to stop swearing when I do."

On struggling with the rhythm in a piece:
"I am amazed at how I ever learned to walk."

AWARD for PERSEVERANCE at a PIANO LESSON

After surviving her piano lesson in which she alternated working on her piano pieces with trips outside in the pouring rain to take pictures of her defective, oh-so-flat NEW tire and meet with the AAA tow truck driver TWICE – interspersed with calls to AAA, to the no-good tire dealer, her husband, and her friend to cancel lunch plans.

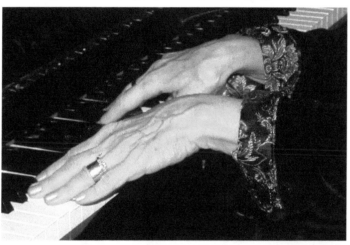

REFERENCES

pages 6–7
Dr. Shinichi Suzuki
Nurtured by Love: The Classic Approach to Talent Education (1993) Pub. Suzuki Method International

Ability Development from Age Zero (1981) Pub. Suzuki Method International

pages 7–8
Dr. Oliver Sacks, *Musicophilia: Tales of Music and the Brain* (2008) Pub. Vintage

"Musical Minds", an episode of the PBS series Nova

Other books not referred to in the text:
Daniel J. Levitin, *This Is Your Brain on Music: The Science of a Human Obsession* (2007) Pub. Plume/Penguin

Aniruddh D. Patel, *Music, Language, and the Brain* (2010) Pub. Oxford University Press

page 21
Divan Orchestra
https://en.wikipedia.org/wiki/West%E2%80%93Eastern_
Divan_Orchestra
https://west-eastern-divan.org/
https://www.youtube.com/watch?v=rGg3nrqSLlI

page 22
Robert Frost, "The Road Not Taken" (1915)
https://www.poetryfoundation.org/poems/44272/the-
road-not-taken
https://en.wikipedia.org/wiki/The_Road_Not_Taken

page 27
Here is one such example of a concert pianist's musical
genealogy: Claudio Arrau

"And so, at the age of 11, Arrau arrived in Germany,
where he began studies with Martin Krause at the Stern
Conservatoire in Berlin.... The musical lineage can be
traced – through Krause-Liszt-Czerny-Beethoven – and it
must not be thought that this is some kind of sentimental
gimmick, a mere combination of circumstances that has
no musical value other than to pedants, for it can surely
be no coincidence that Arrau's international reputation as
a leading interpreter of Beethoven is the result of his own
response to this pedigree."

https://www.princeton.edu/~gpmenos/C_Arrau_at_85.html

page 60
Chopin Frederic Chopin recordings by Arthur Rubinstein
Other notable Chopin performers in alphabetical order
(to mention a few):

Claudio Arrau
Vladimir Ashkenazy
Alfred Cortot
Dinu Lipatti
Maurizio Pollini
Sviatoslav Richter

page 63
"Seven Functions of Language"
https://www.psychologydiscussion.net/social-psycholo-
gy-2/language/7-main-functions-of-language-forms-hu-
man-behaviour-psychology/3145

page 81
When I began writing about Authenticity, my thoughts
turned to Reverend Gilbert E. Fleer, the campus minister
of decades ago who first brought this word to my attention.
https://www.nwaonline.com/obituaries/2020/feb/23/rev-
gilbert-fleer-2020-02-23/

RISK – PENETRATION – AUTHENTICITY
were the key words of Gil's ministry and message during
his days as Methodist Campus Minister in Columbia,
Missouri 1964 – 1967. My memory of these words has
been kept alive or at least made more vivid because I put

those words to a tune that we sang to honor him when he was leaving to take a job in Texas. (If you want to remember something, put the words to music!)

page 103
Psychology Today blog
posted August 11, 2019 by Marilyn A. Mendoza, Ph.D.
"The Power of Music at the End of Life"
https://www.psychologytoday.com/us/blog/understand-ing-grief/201908/the-power-music-the-end-life#:~:tex-t=Research%20into%20the%20use%20of,slow%20and%20deepen%20their%20breath.

ENDORSEMENTS

"This lovely book is a joy to read and a true inspiration. It is completely accessible, every word ringing with authenticity. It is deeply considered, researched, experienced, and understood by the author. It is unflinchingly truthful, warm and compelling. It leaves me feeling excited to play more and to listen more and better. It will influence people's lives as well as their music."

— Patty Ochoa,
adult piano student

"The title of this book could be *The Turtle and the Lion, a partnership toward musical mastery, life fulfillment, and sublime happiness.* It is wonderful, magnificent! I felt warm and cozy reading it. The author is truly a master, philosopher and psychologist rolled into one!"

— Anita Dana,
artist and teacher

"The book gives some very wise advice relating to both music and life. (And I laughed so hard at the quotations from the adult piano students.)"

— Georgia J. Graham, M.A.,
volunteer church organist

"This book is such a beautiful achievement and will be a gift to all who read it. Thank you for sharing your true wisdom and the insights of your soul, as well as your practical suggestions, all in an easy and delightful to read manner. It is thought-provoking and uplifting, and just so thoughtfully constructed. I will definitely recommend it to my adult piano students!"

– Kathryn Christensen Lieppman,
professional pianist and piano teacher

"The book is smart, whimsical, caring, and meaningful even to someone who doesn't remember her childhood piano lessons."

– Piper Johnson Cort, fiber artist

CPSIA information can be obtained
at www.ICGtesting.com
Printed in the USA
BVHW021009180122
626439BV00023B/663

9 781737 818410